# ABC's $
## — OF —
# MONEY

*ABC's of Money*

Copyright © 2020 Karen Jordan. All Rights Reserved.

No rights claimed for public domain material, all rights reserved. No parts of this publication may be reproduced, stored in any retrieval system, or transmitted in any form or by any means, electronic, mechanical, recording, or otherwise, without the prior written permission of the author. Violations may be subject to civil or criminal penalties.

Unless stated otherwise, all Scriptures are taken from the King James Version of the Holy Bible.

ISBN: 978-1-63308-611-1 (paperback)
       978-1-63308-612-8 (ebook)

Cover and Interior Design by *R'tor John D. Maghuyop*

1028 S Bishop Avenue, Dept. 178
Rolla, MO 65401

Printed in United States of America

"Your ears shall hear a word behind you, saying, 'This is the way, walk in it,' Whenever you turn to the right hand or whenever you turn to the left."

**Isaiah 30:21 (NKJV)**

KAREN JORDAN

CHALFANT ECKERT

PUBLISHING

# Table of Contents

| | | | | | | |
|---|---|---|---|---|---|---|
| **A** | Above all Things!! | 7 | | **N** | Need | 34 |
| **B** | Believe!! | 9 | | **O** | Owe no one anything | 36 |
| **C** | Create | 11 | | **P** | Power | 38 |
| **D** | Dead | 13 | | **Q** | Questions and Answers | 40 |
| **E** | Exceedingly!! | 15 | | **R** | Repent | 42 |
| **F** | Faith!! | 17 | | **S** | Swear not | 44 |
| **G** | Greediness | 19 | | **T** | Tithing | 46 |
| **H** | Haughty? | 21 | | **U** | Saved to the uttermost! | 48 |
| **I** | Imitation? Fake, counterfeit | 23 | | **V** | Voice | 50 |
| **J** | Jesus Taught | 25 | | **W** | Walk | 53 |
| **K** | Knowledge | 27 | | **X** | EXalt the Lord your God! | 55 |
| **L** | Love | 30 | | **Y** | Yes! | 57 |
| **M** | Makes | 32 | | **Z** | Zacchaeus | 59 |

# [A] Above all Things!!

> 3 John 2 says, "*Beloved, I wish above all things that thou mayest prosper and be in health, even as thy soul prosper.*" KJV

What do you desire above all things? What do you want the most for, and out of your life? No matter your answer, there is a process and a "doing" on your part.

In today's world, money speaks, and money is needed to survive. God knows we need money to make it, and He has provided truths from the Bible (His Word) for us to read, process, learn, believe, and live.

God is the ultimate "above all!"

He was, He is, and He will always be. Time cannot contain Him, and man cannot change Him. His truths are just that – TRUTH – they will always be available to the person who seeks truth. So, this book is a journey seeking truth about money.

What does it mean to prosper above all things? Webster's Dictionary says it means "to succeed in an enterprise or activity, especially to achieve economic success." God wants us to prosper! He wants us to be successful! He wants us to get on the right path – the path to *success*!

If you are poor, addicted, lonely, sad, sick, depressed, desperate, disappointed, and ready to give up, you need God and His truths. He wants you to have all you need and more than enough!

Philippians 4:19 says, *"And my God shall supply all your need according to His riches in glory by Christ Jesus."*

**So, A is above all things prosper and be in health as your soul prospers.**

# [ B ]
# Believe!!

> Mark 11:22-24 says, *"So Jesus answered and said to them, 'Have faith in God. For assuredly, I say to you, whoever says to this mountain, "Be removed and be cast into the sea," and does not doubt in his heart, but believes that those things he says will be done, he will have whatever he says. Therefore I say to you, whatever things you ask when you pray, believe that you receive them, and you will have them.'"*

Wow! What a truth to read about and decide if we believe it or not. What do you believe about money? What do you believe about your life and if you should have money?

Money is what people use to exchange for what they need. If you live on the earth, you need money!

The devil wants you to believe you are stuck where you are. He wants you to believe you will never have enough, you will never be whole, you will never receive healing, and you will never be happy.

On the other hand, God wants you to believe you can have enough, actually more than enough! He wants you to believe you can be, and are, complete and whole in Him. God wants you to believe you can be, and are, healed. He wants you to believe happiness is for you! He wants you to believe you are unique. There is no one else like you that has ever been created and living on the earth. You were created for a reason and born because you are special!! He is the God of *ALL*!! Why wouldn't He want you to have all?? He doesn't want you to be in need, or to be in lack of, or to struggle for money. Do you believe that? Sometimes, the money struggle has to do with what we believe. You can change your beliefs today by reading the Bible, His Word, and accepting the grace of God through Jesus' death and resurrection to give us prosperous lives on the earth.

## So, B is believe what God says about prosperity and faith to walk in it!

# [ C ]
# Create

*Psalm 51:10 says, "Create in me a clean heart, O God, and renew a steadfast spirit within me." The Passion translation of the Bible says, "Create a new, clean heart within me. Fill me with pure thoughts and holy desires, ready to please you."*

When God creates, like in Genesis, He makes something out of nothing. We are made in His image, and we have the same power to create something from nothing.

Our heart says a lot about us. Jesus told His followers in Matthew 6:21, *"For where your treasure is, there your heart will be also."*

We are not to set our hearts on anything but God and His promises!! I am not to set my heart on getting money but on God and believing He wants me to prosper above all things! If my heart is wrong or set on the wrong things, God has a way for me to renew or change my heart. That is what King David was asking for in Psalm 51. He needed God to change his heart. Paul needed his heart changed in Acts 9. The Apostle Paul was born Saul into a religious Jewish family. He went to school and learned the law. He followed it to the point of dragging and committing good, Christ-followers to their deaths. Saul needed a new heart!! We have no choice when it comes to who we are born to and the environment we are raised in. But, when we begin to learn and realize we have needs, we can take control of our lives and change! God has provided the way, the Bible, for us to use as a manual to create change in our lives. When God creates a clean, new heart in you, you can believe Him that He will prosper and bless you!! You can't create money, but you can create change to believe God's promises about money!

Make sure the words you speak are 'truth' words and not 'lack' words. Because your words create your reality.

**So, C is create your life.**

# [D]
# Dead

*Ephesians 2:1 says, "And you He made alive, who were dead in trespasses and sins."*

The good news is He made us alive!! And He doesn't leave us where we are dead! What does it mean, though, to be dead in trespasses and sins?

The word sin in Greek is *hamartia*. It means literally, "missing the mark," failure, offense, taking the wrong course, wrongdoing, sin, or guilt.

If you are in need, lack, debt, or emotional distress, you are probably dead in your trespasses and sins.

When God, through Moses, led His people out of Egypt, He later gave them rules and laws and the curses of disobedience. In Deuteronomy 28:15-68, God tells them these curses. Verse 15 says, *"But it shall come to pass, if you do not obey the voice of the Lord your God, to observe carefully all His commandments and statutes which I command you today, that all these curses will come upon you and overtake you."*

God is a good God, and He does not curse anybody. We curse ourselves when we do not follow Him in doing what is right!

Think of ways you have misused money – maybe you waste it on things you know you shouldn't do or have; perhaps you love money, or maybe you blame people who have money. Regardless you do not have to be dead about money.

Money is what we use on the earth for exchange, so it is a need. God supplies our needs, according to Philippians 4:19. If you have sinned about money – let's say you have bad credit, you can repent and ask God to create a new heart within you. You can read the Bible and know how to change, so you are blessed and not under the curse!

Money or your need for money should not control you. God wants you to have dominion over the earth, over ALL! Over money! Taking the right course is life and taking the wrong path is death. You get to choose – life or death? Blessing or curse?

**So, D is dead or alive; it's up to you?**

# [E]
# Exceedingly!!

Ephesians 3:20 says, *"Now unto Him who is able to do exceedingly abundantly above all that we ask or think, according to the power that works in us."* NKJV

Webster's says exceedingly means "to an extreme degree"!! God is able to prosper us to an extreme degree!! Beyond what we ask or think!!

But change begins with something new – a new idea, a new book, a new love, a new food, etc. Our world needs CHANGE, where money is concerned! We need change!! Our God is above all! Psalm 57:5 says, *"Be exalted, O God, above the heavens; let your glory be above all the earth."* NKJV

God says in Psalm 50:10, *"For every beast of the forest is mine, and the cattle on a thousand hills."* NKJV

Everything was created by Him and given to man to enjoy. So, our above all God grants us to have all to enjoy. Money is one of the ways God can prosper us or bless us. Blessed in Hebrew, *ashar*, means happy, blessed, prosperous, successful, straight, right, and contented.

It's hard to wrap our heads around exceedingly abundantly. Our world has gone to an extreme degree of hate and wickedness and crime and doing wrong, so to imagine life like God has promised He can give us seems unreal or unbelievable. That's why it is so important to read the Word of God, the Bible.

Only the Word of God can build our faith to make us believe God is good, and He is able to give us what we need and more! Don't you want to live in such a place that you have no need or lack? A place where you can enjoy all things? In Ephesians 3:20, the last part says, "according to the power working in you." What power is that? The power of the resurrection!! The greatest power of all – the dead raised to life!! I would call that a very extreme degree – exceedingly abundantly. The sky is the limit where our blessing is concerned – and really, there is no limit!

## So, E is what do you need to an extreme degree? Exceedingly abundantly?

# [ F ]
# Faith!!

> Hebrews 11:1 says, *"Now faith is the substance (or realization) of things hoped for, the evidence or confidence of things not seen."* NKJV

Wow!! I would say that money can often be something needed and not seen. Money can be something we find ourselves hoping to gain. So, what if that is where you are today? Romans 10:17 says, *"So then faith comes by hearing, and hearing by the Word of God."* NKJV

If you are in need, the Word of God, the Bible, tells us to have faith in God. Mark 11:22 says, *"We have faith in Him to know how to pray and trust Him to fulfill our need."* The only way to have faith and to know is to be in the Bible, the Word of God!!

Faith is a gift given to all men and women who receive Jesus as their Savior, according to Romans 12:3. Then there is a gift of faith given by the Holy Spirit. There is also an increase in faith, and that comes through the Bible. God, our Creator, wants our faith to increase. He wants us to know what He has said to us and what He has promised us. He wants us to rely on Him and pray according to His Word, which is His will.

If you're struggling today with faith, maybe your true struggle is with love? In Galatians 5:6, Paul tells us that faith works through love. Without God's love – *agape* – faith cannot work. An example would be you need healing, and you expect God and others to provide that for you to the point where you're mad at them if you don't get better – that's not love – faith can't work. But, if you get in love, you know only God can supply your need, and you get in the Word for a scripture to stand on and put a smile on your face because you can stand on the truth!! The same with money – it is a form of exchange for what is needed! And Philippians 4:19 tells me God shall supply all my need according to His riches in glory. My faith is in Him!! I refuse to go based on bad experiences or other's doubts or what the world says. I will stand in love, on His Word alone!

**So, F is faith walking in love produces results!!**

# [G]
# Greediness

*1 Timothy 6:10 says, "For the love of money is a root of all kinds of evil, for which some have strayed from the faith in their greediness, and pierced themselves through with many sorrows."* NKJV

Webster's says greed is "a selfish and excessive desire for more of something than is needed." I think greediness, in terms of money, is having a need, getting it fulfilled, and still feeling a need for more money, all the while, the excess money is used for lustful and selfish gain. Many ministers of the Bible throughout time have had lots and lots of money – they were wealthy individuals. However, there is a difference in having a lot and using it to try and fill evil desires, versus having a lot and taking care of others and being a conduit for needs in the body of Christ. We all need money in today's world – that's a fact. How is it supposed to come to us? In Ephesians 2:10, Paul was telling followers of Jesus that we are God's workmanship or poem, and we are created in Christ Jesus for good works, which God prepared beforehand that we should walk in them.

Being a part of a family and knowing your place is a good work. You have a choice to walk in that or not. Providing for your family is a good work – you get to choose to walk in that.

Ministering from the broken places you are healing from, are good works, and you get to decide whether you walk in them or not. If you choose not to walk in good works, you are choosing selfishness and greed. It's like hoarding all the good in your life for only you. Eventually, the streams of getting in your life will dry up, and there will be barrenness – a nothingness – a place in need of change – a place to confess and repent of greed so restoration can happen. You cannot love money and walk in love and faith, so when you love money, it leads you away from the faith, the faith of and in God, and it leads you to great sorrow, sadness, and lack.

**So, G is don't practice greediness but GIVE, GIVE, GIVE, especially the good works God prepared for you!!**

# [H]
# Haughty?

1 Timothy 6:17 says, *"Command those who are rich in this present age not to be haughty, nor to trust in uncertain riches but in the living God, who gives us richly all thing to enjoy."* NKJV

Do you see the world and all that is in it? Can you see the world as a stage that is yours to enjoy? Is it easy to see others up on that stage, having all things? God tells you that all things are for you to enjoy! Get up on that stage and take possession, by faith that works through love, so you can have all things to enjoy! God is the only creator – He created everything for His creation to enjoy!! That means you!!

I think Paul wrote those words to Timothy in 6:17 so people who have a lot, people who are rich in one thing or another would not be proud, they would not be show-offs, they would not feel superior or not have contempt for others because others aren't rich in what they are at the moment. Their haughtiness caused them to trust in their provisions and not trust in God. What do you think happened when they began to trust in their provision instead of their Creator?

Yep, you got it – they lost their riches – they lost their provision – they fell from grace. Galatians 5:1-6 talks about standing in liberty obtained for us by Christ and given to us freely by grace! If you trust in your efforts or the riches themselves, you fall from the gift given to you.

Prosperity and blessing are gifts. They are gifts given to us by God. We can receive them and walk in them or not. The Declaration of Independence says, "We hold these truths to be self-evident, that all men are created equal, that they are endowed by their Creator with certain unalienable Rights, that among these are Life, Liberty, and the pursuit of Happiness." By George, I believe our founders got it!! God has given men certain things, and they are rights of ours – what we do with that truth is up to us and whether we are blessed by His provision all the days of our lives.

**So, H is if you find yourself haughty, repent, and be restored to your unalienable rights.**

# [ 1 ]

# Imitation? Fake, counterfeit

> Romans 12:2 says, *"Stop imitating the ideals and opinions of the culture around you, but be inwardly transformed by the Holy Spirit through a total reformation of how you think. This will empower you to discern God's will as you live a beautiful life, satisfying and perfect in His eyes."* TPT

What does it mean to be imitating or faking where money is concerned? How about flaunting what you have? Or pretending like you have it when you don't? The world we live in places #1 priority on getting money so you can have the things you want. God tells us to transform on the inside. That comes by allowing the Holy Spirit and the Bible to work together to change our desires. We need money, but our #1 priority should be our thoughts set on God and how He wants us to walk in the ways He has prepared for us.

When we set our thoughts on Him and read the Bible, we are empowered to discern God's will for our lives. Remember, the world's a stage, and God has given us all things to enjoy!! The stage is set beautifully for everybody!! The provision from God is satisfying and perfect for us!! We will not see life this way if we imitate the way of the world or culture around us. There is such an emptiness in the world today and such barrenness that God never intended for His creation. His will was enjoyment and satisfaction. If you find yourself imitating or faking your way through life, please stop and listen for the voice, the direction of your Creator. He speaks through the Bible; He speaks through others; He speaks through the Holy Spirit inside you – that inner voice! Proverbs talks about the wisdom of God and the fact that wisdom is always speaking. God won't leave you on your own – trying to figure out what is true and real. He is always available with the power to help you live beautifully!!

**So, I is for don't imitate or be fake like the culture but be real!**

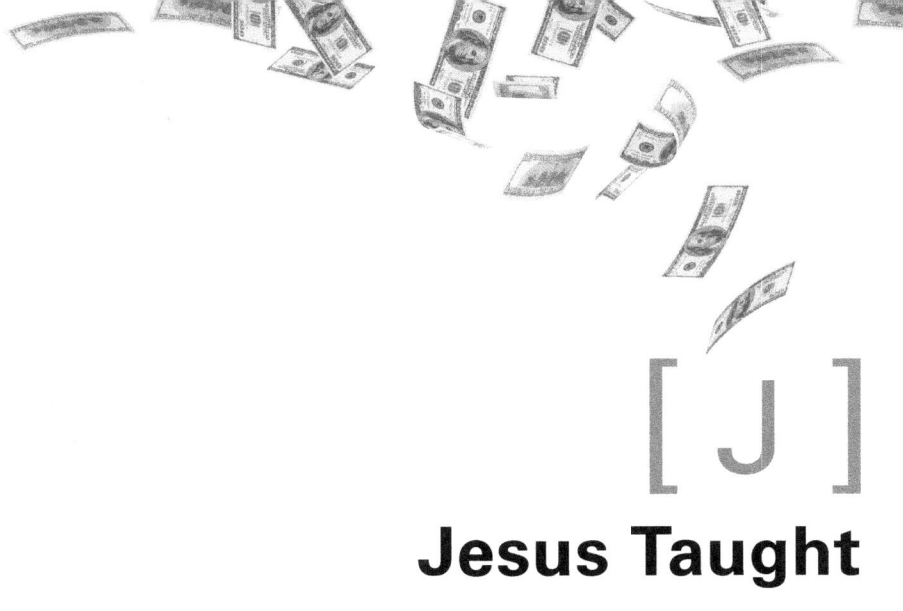

# [ J ]
# Jesus Taught

1. Matthew 25: 14-30 - "The Parable of the Talents" NKJV
2. Matthew 17:24-27 - "Peter and Jesus Pay Their Taxes" KJV
3. Mark 12:41-44 - "The Widow's offering" NKJV
4. Luke 19:11-27 - "The Parable of the Minas" NKJV

Jesus said in John 5:19-23 that He could do nothing of Himself. He said what He saw the Father do, He did. Jesus stayed in an intimate relationship with God, His Father. Obviously, God wanted people to know what He thought about money because Jesus addressed money, and then it was recorded in the Gospels. If Jesus said it, He learned it from God, His Father. So, let's talk about what Jesus taught.

1. The parable of the talents is about how you should take care of the money that you have. Money is a tool to take care of your needs, and when you get money, you should not waste it. Pray and ask God how to increase the money you get – there is a way to do so.

2. Jesus paid His taxes!! Jesus believed in submitting to authority, and He taught His followers to respect where money comes from and to give your share of tax money or where money is due. I believe within this thought is also pay your bills. Money is the means on the earth to exchange something for what we need.

3. Jesus taught that giving to God was important. To give with a cheerful heart is imperative. 2 Corinthians 9:6-8 (NKJV), says *"But this I say, He who sows sparingly will also reap sparingly, and he who sows bountifully (or with blessings) will also reap bountifully (or with blessings). So let each one give as he purposes in his heart, not grudgingly or of necessity; for God loves a cheerful giver. And God is also to make all grace abound toward you, that you, always having all sufficiency in all things, may have an abundance for every good work."* God is looking to see the motive of your heart, not the amount we have to give or the amount we give. I believe it is - Do we want to give it all to Jesus? **Gladly give ALL?**

4. Another parable about receiving money and the expectation about how we will take care of it is the parable of the Minas. Jesus said in the parable in Luke 19:13 "Do business till I come." How are you doing business with what you have? Then we are judged in this parable if we are faithful, even with a very little. Money is a means to take care of us – a way to see our obedience, our motives, our faith, and our generosity.

## So, J is Jesus taught about money. Learn from Him!! He is the Way, the Truth, and the Life!!

# [ K ]
# Knowledge

Proverbs 1:7 says, *"How then does a man gain the essence of wisdom? We cross the threshold of true knowledge when we live in obedient devotion to God. Stubborn know-it-alls will never stop to do this, for they scorn true wisdom and knowledge."* TPT

What is knowledge? The Merriam Webster Dictionary says it is "the fact or condition of knowing something with familiarity gained through experience or association."

How much knowledge do you have where money is concerned? Have you ever learned how to earn it? Save it? Spend it? Not let it control you?

Most people know of money through their home life. How our parents handled and thought of money is a large part of our current situation. Also, classes in school may be part of our knowledge. *BUT*, the greatest knowledge source would be God! His ways and thoughts are high above ours, but He longs to share what He knows with us. It is just a matter of us taking the time to ask Him! God cares about every aspect of our lives! He would absolutely care about our knowledge of money. He knows we need to have money, and He knows we need to understand how to use it.

In all the research done to write this book, the knowledge of God about money can be summed up in 10 quick facts or truths:

1. God cares if we have money and how we see it.

2. Money is the means of trade and living in the earth today. God expects people to work.

3. Jesus taught us by example and through what He heard from God.

4. Love of money is the greatest root of **all** kinds of evils.

5. Jesus taught His disciples to pay their taxes and debtors.

6. Jesus taught His disciples to save money and let it work for them to increase.

7. God cares about prosperity, and being wealthy can be a huge part of prosperity!

8. When in need of money, pray and ask God for HELP!!

9. When in need – **GIVE**. I have heard the phrase: *When in need – sow a seed!* I like that!!

10. God loves His family, and He sees people as a community or a body of believers. Get into a fellowship of people to help carry your load.

If you lack in the area of money, I would suggest to gain knowledge.

**So, K is knowledge – DO NOT be a stubborn know-it-all!!**

# [ L ]
# Love

1 Peter 4:8 says, *"Above all, constantly echo God's intense love for one another, for love will be a canopy over a multitude of sins."* TPT

How does love fit with money? Easy. God, in His infinite wisdom, tells us that love is the most important thing!! We are to love God, love ourselves, love others, and walk in love. If money is a means to trade and have, it makes sense that God would have us use money to love others! I believe we see love demonstrated the most at Christmas time. People use their money, time, and resources to bless others and bring them comfort and enjoyment.

John 3:16 says that God so **loved** the world that He gave – He gave us Jesus, our Savior. I think that is a great litmus test. If we so love the world and others, what do we give? What are we willing to give? Sometimes all we have to offer is love! Other times we can give out of the abundance we have, or we can give **all** we have, like the widow who dropped her two mites in the treasury while Jesus and His disciples were watching. Jesus said she put in more than even the rich who were giving a lot. I think Jesus was sitting opposite the treasury and watching because He was going to use this opportunity to teach His disciples more about money. He always had deeper meanings, and He always taught them about motives.

The Apostle Paul also taught us in the book of Acts, verses 20:33-35, that you are not to covet or lust after anyone's money or clothing or anyone's anything, but you are to labor and give. In verse 35, he says that giving brings a far greater blessing than receiving. Love is all about giving! God's love is a giving thing. He doesn't just speak empty words, instead He follows what He says with action. We are to follow His lead!

Money, again, is just a means to an end, and we are to use it to love God, love ourselves, and love others! Jesus taught that the greatest commandment for us was *love*. In all my days on earth, I realize that I cannot out-give God and that as I give, out of love, He gives me back more than I can imagine!

## So, L is love. Being successful at money begins and ends with love!!

# [M]
## Makes

Proverbs 10:22 says, *"The blessing of the Lord makes one rich, and He adds no sorrow with it."* NKJV

What do you make? When I read this verse in light of money, I think about how I live and treat others. The blessing of the Lord is His promises to us; it's His prosperity becoming ours; it's our lives lived like His and full of joy! What does my life story make in others' lives?

*M* is about conscious intentions of making our lives a witness to God's. His promise to us is that His blessing will make us rich, and He, God, will add no sorrow with it! We are made in His image, and we are to walk in good works that He has prepared for us to accomplish. I want my walk and way and blessing to make others rich! I don't want to add sorrow to anyone.

We can also look at the word "makes" and think about making wages, making grades, making others happy, making the world a better place. What are you working on making? If I go to work to "make money," I will be working for money, and I am not so sure I will enjoy it or do what is right with it. But, if my thought is I am going to work to "make others rich," I will have a totally different attitude and motive. Money will come to me as a resource to add to my life and others' lives and to add to the Kingdom of God. Stop and meditate on this:

_____blessing makes others rich and
      (your name)

_____adds no sorrow to others.
      (your name)

You are important and you make a difference in this world! We all walk together, and if we think of God and others while we think of money, our hearts will be changed to be like His! **Made** in **His image**! I pray we all bless others and make others rich, and we add no sorrow to the world. What are you making today?

## So, M is makes – what do you make?

# [N]
# Need

Philippians 4:19 says, *"And my God shall supply all your need according to His riches in glory by Christ Jesus."* NKJV

We all need! Are you in need? The Apostle Paul was very open about his and others' needs, including money or financial support. In Philippians 4:10-20, Paul talks of his needs and how the Philippian Church shared their money with him. Over and over again, that church met Paul's needs, and out of his gratitude to God and them, he blessed them with the promise that the fruit they were seeking would be added to their account, and God would supply all their need. That tells me if I need an investment yielding spiritual fruit or any other need, I must give. It also tells me that everybody has needs.

1 John 3:17 says if we see a fellow believer in need and do nothing, how is it possible God's love lives in us? The Passion Translation explains that love is action, not just talk – love is like a verb instead of a noun. *All* people have needs, and if we find someone in need,

and we have the means to help, God's love in us will compel us to meet their needs.

I believe this is challenging, so you must pray how to help others, because there is also a lot of manipulation and using that goes on as well. God, in His faithfulness can lead you.

I see needs everywhere, but I know the God of more than enough! It is so imperative to *know* God through His Word! If you have a deep understanding of His Word, you will find the answers to your needs in the Word.

I also believe that in need, first, ask God what is most important and what may be frivolous that you don't need. Sometimes we end up in need because we are used to living a certain way and depending on men to supply everything we want and need. There is a big difference between want and need. Needs are things like food, water, air to breathe, sleep, and money to pay our bills. Wants are things like a new car, new clothes, or the latest gadget everybody else has. God knows what we NEED vs. what we WANT! And His Word says He supplies!! Have you ever had a need met that was a miracle? Take some time to think of all the needs God has supplied for you, then be grateful for His supply, His truth, and His care for you and yours.

**So, N is need – surrender all your needs to the Almighty God, who is more than enough to supply them!**

# [o]

# Owe no one anything

> Romans 13:8 says, *"Owe no one anything except to love one another, for he who loves another has fulfilled the law."*

God's Word to us is to owe "1" thing – LOVE! I can imagine a world where that is the standard – heaven? But, if we couldn't accomplish owing only love, why would God ask us to owe only that? I have to believe He knew we could do it!!

I have read a lot on love lately, and one of the statements I thought was great is to see love as a verb instead of a noun. It is an action and not just a thing. Love can take on many faces and deeds. Love could be a warm meal for a sick friend. Love could be babysitting someone's children. Love could be helping your neighbor with their project. Love could be a smile on a long journey. Love could be a word of encouragement to someone who is sick, dying, or brokenhearted. Love can be visiting someone in prison. Love can be a simple hug or a complex backrub. Love can be attentiveness – listening to someone who needs to talk. Love can be cheering someone on in whatever they need! Love can be a card or a gift bought with that person in mind. Love can be putting others before yourself. Love can be biting your tongue and not answering in anger or sarcasm. Love can be a kind word to a total stranger. Love can be buying someone's meal and paying it forward. Love is praying to God for others and for His will to be accomplished on the earth!

There are lots of ways to give the one thing (love) God tells us to owe. I think God is pretty amazing for giving us directions about love. In 1 Corinthians 13, "the love chapter" of the Bible, we are told what love is and isn't. In 1 John 4:8, we are also told that God is love. So, God is telling us we owe no man anything except to be like God to them!! You can do this!! You were created in God's image to carry out His plan for this universe. You are important to God!

**So, O is owe LOVE!! If you do have debts, surrender those to God and have Him help you to pay them off in LOVE!!**

# [ P ]
# Power

*"Behold, I send the Promise of my Father upon you; but tarry in the city of Jerusalem until you are endued with power from on high."* Luke 24:49 (NKJV)

Jesus told His disciples to wait and then go in the power of God, that was given to us when Christ died. That resurrection power is in us through and by the Holy Spirit! What are you waiting for? I believe God would say, "Don't move too soon." Move when you are filled with power! There are four "power" words in the Bible. This one here is *dunamis*, and it means energy, power, might, great force, great ability, and strength. Dynamite comes from this word. So, the power you are waiting on is hugely explosive and able to help you and get you through!! Financial and money woes are scary, and they seem never-ending and overwhelming, but there is a power from God that is meant for us. It is for us to use in faith, believing that debt is under our feet, and we stand on promises!! In Acts 1:8, the resurrected Jesus told His followers again, that they would receive power when the Holy Spirit comes upon them and they would be witnesses to the world!

The world system we live in and are under is all about money and power. The assumption is if you have money, you have power, and sometimes that is true, but according to Jesus, if you have the Holy Spirit, you have power. Power to rule and reign over your circumstances. Power to be the head and not the tail. In the book of Deuteronomy, in chapter 28, Moses records what God tells him about blessings to those who obey. Verse 13 says, *"And the LORD, Jehovah, will make you the head and not the tail, you shall be above only, and not be beneath, if you heed the commandments of the LORD your God, which I command you today, and are careful to observe them."* As redeemed people by the blood of Jesus, our commandments is love. In John 13:34, Jesus says, *"A new commandment I give to you, that you love one another; as I have loved you, that you also love one another."* So, when we obey God by loving, we will walk in power!! Choose to follow Jesus and submit to His authority today. You will receive and walk in more blessings than you can count. One of those blessings is power – power to change the course of your life with debts and money. Surrender to Him and His Power!!

**So, P is power – all power is Christ's because He died for it – when we receive Him as Savior, it becomes ours!**

# [Q]

# Questions and Answers

> Luke 2: 46-47 says, *"Now so it was that after three days they found Him in the temple, sitting in the midst of the teachers, both listening to them and asking them questions. And all who heard Him were astonished at His understanding and answers."*

God has, and is, all the answers to every question. There is nothing new in your life that He doesn't already know and have an answer for! He longs to have a relationship with you. A relationship filled with conversation – questions and answers. No question is too small or dumb, and no answer will condemn you.

God loves you dearly. He longs to take all your questions and answer them in a way you understand and in a way that you will trust Him for your life.

This book is about money, so how does that relate to questions and answers? I think we all need help where money is concerned. I am sure you have questions about how to get it, how to spend it, how to save it, and how not to let money be what you love. God has the answers to those questions, first and foremost in His Word, the Bible. Secondly, through prayer – when you pray, you are having a conversation with God. Do you expect Him to answer? Do you expect to hear His reply? You should, because His wisdom is always speaking! Proverbs 8:1 says, *"Does not wisdom cry out, and understanding lift up her voice?"*

Verse 6 says, *"Listen, for I will speak of excellent things, and from the opening of my lips will come right things;"*

There are so many places in Proverbs where wisdom, God's wisdom, is speaking to us! Thirdly, He answers us through others – maybe a pastor, maybe a financial advisor, maybe a spouse, or maybe just a friend.

Last but not least, knowledge. If you are having problems with your money and you need help, educate yourself. Proverbs 1:5 says, *"A wise man will hear and increase learning, And a man of understanding will attain wise counsel."*

Sometimes we have to put down our pride and humble ourselves to ask for help with money or financial issues, but God loves a humble and contrite heart – He loves to answer the person who is honest and comes with questions and is seeking for God's answer.

**So, Q is for questions – Ask away – no question is too small or too big. God knows everything, and He is so ready to go to work on your behalf!**

# [ R ]
# Repent

Revelation 3:19 says, *"All those I dearly love I unmask and train. So repent and be eager to pursue what is right."* TPT

If your life is in shambles and you feel like you are at the end of your rope, there is a Savior; His name is Jesus Christ, the Messiah, the Anointed One, and His Anointing. He longs for you to cast your care on Him because He cares for you! 1 Peter 5:7 says He wants you to come to the end of yourself and realize your need for Him! In the Gospel of John chapter 4, John tells a story of a woman at the well. Jesus asks her for a drink, and then He proceeds to have a conversation with her. In His conversation, Jesus tells her that He is the one that can give living water. He has all the answers and can give her all the guidance she needs. She must repent and worship God. Repentance is turning away from all that is wrong in your life. Repentance is giving up bad behaviors, bad thoughts, and bad words. Repentance is realizing depending on yourself is a dead-end street that leads you down dark, dead paths. After repentance comes confession.

Romans 10:9&10 says, *"if you confess with your mouth the Lord Jesus and believe in your heart that God has raised Him from the dead, you will be saved. For with the heart one believes unto righteousness, and with the mouth confession is made unto salvation."*

In the New Spirit-Filled Life Bible, they have a word wealth for repent. It is the Greek word *metanoeo*, and it is a decision that results in a change of mind, which in turn leads to a change of purpose and action.

Romans 3:23 says, *"for all have sinned and fall short of the glory of God."* We are all in need of help!! That help comes from God. Admitting your need and confessing your sin takes courage. God gives us the courage to follow Him and change our minds, our behaviors, our ways, our spending, our hope. God has a path for each one of us, and repentance is a step to get us on the right path. If Jesus is your Savior and your life does not reflect that, you can repent again. Remember, it is a decision that results in change! Good change!!

## So, R is for repent for the Kingdom of Heaven is at hand!

# [s]
# Swear not

> James 5:12 says, *"But above all things, my brethren, swear not, neither by heaven, neither by earth, neither by any other oath: but let your yea be yea; and your nay, nay; lest ye fall into temptation."* KJV

We live in a society with lots of swearing, like swearing seems to make our argument, right? But James, Jesus' brother, tells us to let your yes be yes or your no be no. You don't have to verify by anything other than the truth that comes out of your mouth.

There used to be a time when a man's word, or his oath, was golden, and at all costs, you did not break your promise. Proverbs 22:1a (TPT) says, *"A beautiful reputation is more to be desired than great riches,"*

Jesus told His followers, recorded in Matthew 12:36-37, *"But I say to you that for every idle word men may speak, they will give account of it in the day of judgment. For by your words you will be justified, and by your words you will be condemned."* So, how does not swearing help us deal with money? You have to go to God, either by the Bible, His Word, or through prayers, or counsel and ask for wisdom, knowledge, and understanding for money.

Be careful what comes out of your mouth. Another principle of God is that you get what you say – that's why confession is so important. If you are hurting for money, I suggest you go boldly to the throne of grace so you can obtain mercy and find grace in your time of need. Hebrews 4:16.

Tell God the truth of where you are and the fact that you need His help! You do not need to swear by anything. He already knows. Then, what you say after going to the throne and confessing is *so* vital to your financial freedom. If you confess you don't have enough, that is what you will get. So, be knowledgeable of what is yours in the Bible. What are the promises that you can claim and stand on concerning your financial needs? If every one of your words condemns you or justifies, and you believe that then I would think you would be a person of little words and certainly not a person who would swear.

**So, S is swear not – let your yes be yes, and your no be no.**

# [T]
# Tithing

Genesis 14:20b says, *"And he gave him a tithe (one-tenth) of all."*

Tithing is giving to God one-tenth of all you have or earn. It is first mentioned in the book of Genesis when Abram returns from rescuing his nephew, Lot, and others, and Abram is fed and blessed by Melchizedek, king of Jerusalem. After Melchizedek blesses him, Abram gives him a tenth of all. I believe the principle of God we are to take away from this first mention is when we follow and obey God, even when it looks like imminent danger, or death, there is a blessing you receive. And out of the blessing from God, you give back.

I first learned to tithe when I was 18 and a single mother. I did not have much, but I learned that God had blessed me with life, love, peace, and happiness, and my return to show Him my devotion and love was to give a tithe.

Some people give their lives to the study and teaching of God and His ways. We can learn from them, and we can counsel with them; they are considered our priests or pastors of today, and we see by the example of the Bible that we are to support those in spiritual authority over us by giving the church (the storehouse) our tithe.

I truly believe that you can't stop the blessing when you tithe. Malachi 3:8-12 says, *"'Will a man rob God? Yet you have robbed me! But you say, "In what way have we robbed you?" In tithes and offerings. You are cursed with a curse, For you have robbed me, even this whole nation. Bring all the tithes into the storehouse, That there may be food in my house, And try Me now in this,' Says the Lord of hosts, 'If I will not open for you the windows of heaven And pour out for you such blessing That there will not be room enough to receive it. And I will rebuke the devourer for your sakes, so that he will not destroy the fruit of your ground, Nor shall the vine fail to bear fruit for you in the field.' Says the Lord of hosts; 'And all nations will call you blessed, For you will be a delightful land,' Says the Lord of hosts."*

That is a beautiful picture of what God longs to do for you in the area of your need, and that includes money! He blesses you – you give to Him – and He pours out on you more than you can contain!

## T is for tithe – if you never tried this principle, listen to Malachi and start and see if God is not faithful to help you with your money.

# [U]

# Saved to the uttermost!

> Hebrews 7:25 says, *"Therefore He is also able to save to the uttermost those who come to God through Him, since He always lives to make intercession for them."* NKJV

What does it mean to be saved to the uttermost? Especially where money is concerned? To be saved to the uttermost means to be saved for all time – now and in the future – whatever is needed! Saved to the extreme!! The farthest boundaries! Are you in need of being "saved" where your money is concerned? Are you floundering around and having no hold on how to have enough money to survive and even prosper? Well, the good news is God wants you to be able to make it and even have more than enough!

When we are saved – it is our spirit that is awakened and follows Jesus, then our bodies and souls should follow suit. Remember, we are a spirit, we live in a body, and we have a soul. The health of all three components is up to us!

3 John 2 says, *"Beloved, I pray that you may prosper in all things and be in health, just as your soul prospers."* So it is imperative to know how to have a healthy soul that is saved to the uttermost. Let's fly through the pages of the Bible and go to Romans 12:1-2. It says, *"I beseech you therefore, brethren, by the mercies of God, that you present your bodies a living sacrifice, holy, acceptable to God, which is your reasonable service. And do not be conformed to this world, but be transformed by the renewing of your mind, that you may prove what is that good and acceptable and perfect will of God."* According to 3 John, we can prosper as our soul prospers – our soul is our mind, our will, and our emotions – those **need** to be renewed to God through reading His Word, the Bible.

When your mind is saved to the uttermost, and the extreme, you will have the wisdom to **know** how to make money, you will have the wisdom to know how to spend your money, and you will know how to believe for money. I also love the thought that Jesus lives to make intercession for me. He is always before the throne of God petitioning for me!

## So, U is saved to the uttermost! There is no lack with God through His Son, Jesus!!

# [ v ]
# Voice

Psalm 29 – All of Psalm 29!! God is speaking! He longs to be the voice you listen to about money. He makes His voice known through His Word!

In Psalm 29:1-2, David is giving God what is due Him, which is praise and remembering all His promises.

Verse 3 says, *"The voice of the Lord is over the waters; The God of glory thunders; The Lord is over many waters."* Do you feel as though you're sometimes drowning when it comes to money? Well, according to this Psalm, God's voice is over the waters! Good news!

Verse 4: *"The voice of the Lord is powerful; the voice of the Lord is full of majesty."* There is nothing higher than His Voice! Proclaim out of your mouth what mountains need to move and what finances need to come - do it in His Name! His voice is powerful!

Verse 5 says, *"The voice of the Lord breaks the cedars, yes the Lord splinters the cedars of Lebanon."* His voice splinters the greatest of trees – trees can sometimes represent men or mindsets – ***speak***, speak over your circumstances and tell them to move!! In Jesus Name, is Him speaking through you. He told us in Matthew 28:18 that all authority had been given to Him, and then He gave that authority to us and told us to use our voices for God and good, healing, and wholeness! If He speaks and His voice is powerful, then you inherit the same thing!

Verse 6 says, *"He makes them also skip like a calf, Lebanon and Sirion like a young wild ox."* The Passion Translation says He moves Zion's mountains by the might of His voice!

Verse 7: *"The voice of the Lord divides the flames of fire."* What a promise!! Sometimes you just feel like you're in the midst of a fire, and your money is just getting burned up, but verse 7 says He divides the flames!! Do you remember Shadrach, Meshach, and Abednego and the fire? In Daniel 3:25, the king said, *"I see four men loose, walking in the midst of the fire, and they are not hurt, and the form of the 4th is like the Son of God."* Verse 27 says they weren't even singed, and they didn't smell like fire! WOW!!

Verse 8: *"The voice of the Lord shakes the wilderness; The Lord shakes the wilderness of Kadesh."* Do you often feel alone, in the wilderness, especially about your money? Well, good news, God's voice shakes that aloneness!

Verse 9 says, *"The voice of the Lord makes the deer give birth, And strips the forests bare; And in His temple everyone says, 'Glory!'"* If you are struggling, you need new life to overcome the darkness and start fresh!

Verse 10: *"The Lord sat enthroned at the Flood, and the Lord sits as King forever."* He still was Lord and King during the great flood, and He will be King forever. Worship Him and make Him your Savior and source! He will help you *speak* the right things over your life and your money!

Verse 11: *"The Lord will give strength to His people; the Lord will bless His people with peace."*

Praise the Lord! His voice is for you, and He longs to teach you how to use your voice to be free and whole and to have enough with your money!

## So, V is for voice. He will never be quiet, and He speaks life constantly and forever!

# [W]
# Walk

Isaiah 30:21, *"When you turn to the right or turn to the left, you will hear His voice behind you to guide you, saying this is the right path; follow it."* TPT

Isaiah 30:21 says, **"Your ears shall hear a word behind you, saying, 'This is the way, walk in it,' Whenever you turn to the right hand or whenever you turn to the left."** (NKJV)

Does God really talk to people? My answer is a resounding YES!! I recently watched a movie called "Harriet" about Harriet Tubman, and there is a book named, "The Man Who Talks with Flowers" about George Washington Carver. I would recommend the movie and the book! Both tell stories of fellow Americans who prayed and listened to God for different reasons. God told George Washington Carver the many uses for the peanut, and He helped him with research for crops. God told Harriet Tubman when to turn to the left or right. Both fellow Americans were successful in their field of freedom because they asked God, listened to God, and walked in His way!

This book is about money. God has a way for you to walk that is just right for you in the area of ***your*** money. Every person and every need is significant and unique in the sight of God. He is waiting for us to inquire of Him – ask Him – cry to Him for help in time of need! Hebrews 4:16 says, *"Let us therefore come boldly to the throne of grace, that we may obtain mercy and find grace to help in time of need."*

The steps to knowing how to walk in His ways are to: #1 Inquire or ask, #2 Listen, and #3 Obey. Throughout the entire Bible and the course of history, God has been a constant in the affairs of man. He is ever-present and ready to help. He is just waiting for mankind to engage Him to get involved.

From Adam, the first man, to John the Beloved Apostle, the Bible is full of stories of men and women needing God's help. He was always ready to step in, and He was just waiting for them to ask.

You are no different! He knows your need before you ask Him. He knows the right path for you to walk, and He is waiting for you to engage Him in your life.

**So, W is walk! Walk with God, and He will help you in your time of need.**

# [X]

# EXalt the Lord your God!

> Psalm 99:5 says, *"Exalt the Lord our God, And worship at His footstool – He is holy."*

Exalt means to elevate, raise, bring up, lift up, hold up, extol, to make high and powerful. To exalt God is to lift Him up to the #1 place in our lives. Sometimes it is not easy to do that when the cares of this world are so significant in our lives. When we have a lack of anything, especially money, it is hard to remember that God knows our business, and He wants to help us.

What is first in your life? What is elevated and consumes your thoughts? Jesus told His disciples in Matthew 6:19-21, *"Do not lay up for yourselves treasures on earth, where moth and rust destroy and where thieves break in and steal; but lay up for yourselves in heaven, where neither moth nor rust destroys and where thieves do not break in and steal. For where your treasure is, there your heart will be also."*

If money or things or the concern for money and things is first in your thoughts, then that would be your treasure, and God wants to help you. Later on in the Gospel of Matthew 11:28, Jesus said, *"Come to me, all you who labor and are heavy laden, and I will give you rest."*

Verse 29 says, *"Take my yoke upon you and learn from me, for I am gentle and lowly in heart, and you will find rest for your souls."*

Verse 30: *"For my yoke is easy and My burden is light."* Jesus is the answer, and He has the answer.

Exalt Him above money. Exalt Him above your need. Exalt Him above worry. Exalt Him above your thoughts. He has made you many promises, why not put Him to the test and see if He is faithful and true to His Word?

Jesus said in Matthew 6:33, "*Seek first the kingdom of God and His righteousness, and all these things shall be added to you.*" What things is He talking about in this passage? In the verses above verse 33, He is talking about provision – needs such as food, water, clothing, health.

## So, X is exalt – put Him first, and all the things will be added to you – all your needs, including money.

# [ Y ]
# Yes!

2 Corinthians 1:19 says, *"For the Son of God, Jesus Christ, who was preached among you by us – by me, Silvanus, and Timothy – was not Yes and No, but in Him was Yes."*

What good news that Jesus, when He is preached, is a big resounding **YES**!! Verse 20: *"FOR ALL THE PROMISES OF GOD IN HIM ARE YES, AND IN HIM AMEN, TO THE GLORY OF GOD THROUGH US."*

Everything is a yes, and for all who will believe!

What an amazing God that He would have men, inspired by the Holy Spirit, record who He is and His promises to us in a book. Why would He do that if He didn't mean to keep those promises to us?

He promises you that He will never leave you nor forsake you. He promises you provision. He promises you that healing has been secured for you by the blood of Jesus at Calvary. He promises you redemption through that precious blood. Ephesians 1:7 says, *"In Him we have redemption through His blood."* Redemption is a release secured by the payment of a ransom, deliverance, and setting free.

I think you should go to God today and tell Him what you need – I think you should tell Him how you feel – I think You should see if He keeps His promises. He already knows your needs. Doing good in life is about putting Him first and trusting Him to help you with the rest.

If you need money, tell Him, but be open and willing to hear His answer and obey Him. He might say go to work. He might say save. He might say tithe. He might say give to your neighbor whose need is more significant than yours. Whatever His answer is, it will be YES!!

## So, Y is yes – in Him is yes!!

# [z]
# Zaccheus

> Luke 19:1-10 verse 5 says, *"Zacchaeus, make haste and come down, for today I must stay at your house."*

Zacchaeus was rich in money. When Jesus passed through his town, Zacchaeus longed to see who he was. Zacchaeus was also a wee little man, and a wee little man was he, so he climbed up in a sycamore tree for the Lord he wanted to see. Jesus looked up and saw him and told him to get ready because Jesus was coming to his house. Everybody else in town complained because they believed Zacchaeus to be a sinner because of his job and the fact he was rich. Zacchaeus felt the pressure and judgment of his neighbors, and Jesus' presence also convicted him, so Zacchaeus said he would restore what he might have wrongfully taken, and restore more than that. I believe when he was in the presence of Jesus, his heart changed. That is what happens when we spend time with God, whether in prayer, reading the Bible, or fellowship – our hearts change. Zacchaeus' story is just the story of a rich man, but poor men also can experience this great redemption.

KAREN JORDAN

Jesus told Zacchaeus that Jesus, He, had come to seek and save that which was lost.

We all need this man, Jesus! Rich or poor, black or white, healthy or sick, man or woman, we are going about life, and when the Promise of Peace steps into our presence, we are transformed!! My hope and prayer in this book is that you will invite Jesus into your house and heart and allow Him to change you. He longs to help you. He longs to save you. He longs to show Himself strong on your behalf. He longs to make you rich and bless you. He longs to prosper you!

**So, Z is for Zacchaeus – a man whose story is recorded in the good book. Is your story recorded in heaven as well?**

www.ingramcontent.com/pod-product-compliance
Lightning Source LLC
Chambersburg PA
CBHW050045080526
44586CB00014B/1462